Companion Gardening

A Practical Guide For Beginners To Learn Everything About Companion Planting

Copyright 2015 by Better Life Solutions- All rights reserved.

This document is geared towards providing exact and reliable information in regards to the topic and issue covered. The publication is sold with the idea that the publisher is not required to render accounting, officially permitted, or otherwise, qualified services. If advice is necessary, legal or professional, a practiced individual in the profession should be ordered.

- From a Declaration of Principles which was accepted and approved equally by a Committee of the American Bar Association and a Committee of Publishers and Associations.

In no way is it legal to reproduce, duplicate, or transmit any part of this document in either electronic means or in printed format. Recording of this publication is strictly prohibited and any storage of this document is not allowed unless with written permission from the publisher. All rights reserved.

The information provided herein is stated to be truthful and consistent, in that any liability, in terms of inattention or otherwise, by any usage or abuse of any policies, processes, or directions contained within is the solitary and utter responsibility of the recipient reader. Under no circumstances will any legal responsibility or blame be held against the publisher for any reparation, damages, or monetary loss due to the information herein, either directly or indirectly.

Respective authors own all copyrights not held by the publisher.

The information herein is offered for informational purposes solely, and is universal as so. The presentation of the information is without contract or any type of guarantee assurance.

The trademarks that are used are without any consent, and the publication of the trademark is without permission or backing by the trademark owner. All trademarks and brands within this book are for clarifying purposes only and are the owned by the owners themselves, not affiliated with this document.

Table of Contents

Introduction 4

Chapter 1 – Benefits of Companion Gardening 5

Chapter 2 - Companion Gardening Projects 12

Chapter 3 – Transitioning to a Companion Garden 20

Chapter 4 – Companion Gardening in Perspective 25

Chapter 5 - A Plant-by-Plant Reference Guide 33

Introduction

This book contains proven steps and strategies on how to successfully use companion planting in your own garden to improve the health of your crops.

You will learn which plants can grow together without competing for the same resources, as well as how to use companion planting to reduce pests and improve soil quality. Instead of just being presented with charts and lists, you will find out how to plant and maintain several companion gardening projects from the ground up.

Here Is A Preview Of What You'll Learn...

- The background and history of companion gardening
- Six benefit of companion planting
- How to plant a Three Sisters garden
- How to plant a summer vegetable mini companion garden
- Companion gardening for your patio or balcony
- How to transition your garden to companion planting
- The science of companion planting
- A reference guide to compatible and incompatible plants

Chapter 1 – Benefits of Companion Gardening

What Is Companion Gardening?

Companion planting is the practice of planting different garden species close together, rather than keeping each type of plant in its own specific row or corner of the garden. Different kinds of plants interact with each other and with the natural environment in beneficial ways.

Why Use Companion Gardening?

Thousands of years ago, our ancestors discovered that if they specialized in growing just a few crops, they could increase the amount of food they produced. But planting the same crop year after year in the same field led to problems. Every plant species needs slightly different nutrients, and these get depleted quickly if the same crops are planted successively. Diseases that target specific crops can also be left behind in the soil from season to season. Crop rotation was invented to minimize these negative effects. Farmers across the globe have also known for thousands of years that planting different species in the same area could improve the health and the yields of their crops.

During the Green Revolution in the mid 20th century, farmers all over the world were encouraged to plant newly-developed disease-resistant crops in large monoculture operations. Essentially the same crop would be planted year after year in the same field, with the help of chemical fertilizers, pesticides and agricultural machinery. There's no doubt that this practice fed millions or even billions of people who would have otherwise gone hungry. However, progress has come at a cost. Traditional agricultural practices often create habitat for wild animals and plants, but these are lost with industrial farming. Lack of biodiversity also means lack of nutritional variety, and many people are suffering from malnutrition even though they may consume more calories than before. Pesticides have harmed wild plants and animals, as well as causing health problems such as cancer in humans.

More and more people are turning to traditional gardening and farming techniques as a way to combat these problems. The future of global industrial farming may be too big a problem for you to contend with, but even if you only have a balcony or an urban patio to work with, you can experience the satisfaction of growing a little bit of your own food.

Here are some of the benefits that companion planting can bring to your garden.

Structural Support

Taller, sun-loving plants can provide shade for shorter plants. In West Africa, cocoa farmers plant new trees in the shade of plantain and cassava plants, both of which are also food crops. Planting coffee in the shade of natural forests in Central America and Africa benefits both the coffee crop and the ecosystem.

Companion plants can also act as a living trellis for a climbing plant. Pole beans can climb up cornstalks, and sunflowers or Jerusalem artichokes can act as support for climbing beans, small cucumbers and other vine plants. The traditional Native North American combination of corn, beans and squash, known as the Three Sisters, uses corn as a trellis for beans.

The Three Sisters example also shows another structural use of companion plants – living mulch. The low-growing squash in this grouping helps guard against drying of the soil and helps keep weeds away, just as regular mulch would. Vetch and clover are also frequently used as living mulches.

Nitrogen Fixing

All green plants require nitrogen to grow and survive. Most plants need to use nitrogen that is already in the soil, but a few can take it straight from the atmosphere, and even "fix" it in the soil where other plants can use it. Beans (and all legumes) are nitrogen fixers, which brings us back to the Three Sisters example yet again. Clover, vetch and alfalfa are other good examples of nitrogen-fixing plants. These plants provide a small amount of nitrates to the soil while they are living, but it's after they die and decompose that you get the biggest benefit. This is why nitrogen fixers are often planted at the end of the growing season and plowed into the soil before the new planting. These crops are sometimes called "green manure."

Attracting or Repelling Insects

Some plants seem to keep pests away. Marigolds and alliums (onions and garlic) are often used for this purpose. Other plants are good at attracting beneficial insects to your garden. Asters, cosmos and many other flowers provide a home for insect predators that feed on aphids and other pests. They also bring in pollinators such as bees and butterflies. Trap cropping is another way to use companion plants to control the insects in your garden: you include some plants especially for the insects to eat so that they leave your important plants alone. Nasturtiums are often used to keep aphids and whiteflies away from your garden plants. Planting nightshade can successfully lure certain potato bugs away from your potato plants.

Allelopathy

Allelopathy refers to the ability some plants have to produce chemicals that inhibit the growth of other plants. This is important to companion gardening in two ways. First of all, you can avoid combining crops that interfere with each other. Secondly, you can include plants that inhibit the growth of weeds, reducing the amount of time you have to spend weeding. Asters can inhibit ragweed, and rye grass can help keep a number of aggressive weeds under control.

Increasing Yield

Some plants seem to produce more when they are planted together for reasons that nobody fully understands. Tomatoes and basil don't just taste good together: if you plant them together you may get a better yield from both plants.

There are also less mysterious ways that companion planting can help you increase your yield. If you have a small space, you can plant fast-growing plants like radishes next to slower-growing eggplants or peppers. Plants with shallow roots (such as lettuce) can share space with deep-rooted plants like carrots. This way you can get two crops in the space that you would normally devote to one crop.

Aesthetics

The wild beauty of a companion garden can be an end in itself for many people. Imagine a vegetable garden with a variety of foliage colors and textures side-by-side, and with colorful flowers interspersed, visited by bumblebees and butterflies. Compare this image with monotonous rows of vegetables separated by bare earth (or more likely, weeds) and you'll see why so many people are attracted to companion planting.

Chapter 2 - Companion Gardening Projects

There are endless charts and lists available of garden plants and their various "friends" and "enemies." This is all good information, but it can get pretty overwhelming, and it doesn't give you a good idea of where to start. This book will focus instead on several companion planting projects that you can try, no matter how much or how little experience you have as a gardener.

As with any style of gardening, you will have to prepare the soil and keep your plants supplied with water and fertilizer when necessary.

Keep in mind that there will be some trial and error involved. The interplay between climate, soil, plants and insects in the environment is so complex that it's hard to reduce companion planting to hard and fast rules. This may be the reason that scientific studies haven't yet been able to confirm much about the practical details of companion planting, even though many of the principles behind it are scientifically sound.

A Three Sisters Garden

This is one of the most familiar examples of companion planting. It was used over much of North America by Native American gardeners in order to grow food for winter storage. The squash protect the soil from weeds and from drying out; the corn acts as a trellis for the beans, and the beans fix nitrogen in the soil. It works best if you use flour corn, winter squash and climbing beans, but if you have no interest in growing flour corn, you can probably get away with planting sweet corn instead. In the spirit of companion planting, try including a few different varieties of beans and squash even in this small garden. Scarlet runner and Kentucky wonder are two popular climbing beans; pumpkin, acorn and butternut squash are all familiar winter squash.

With this garden you can harvest everything in the fall and plant the same crops the following year, taking advantage of the nitrogen-fixing properties of the beans. There are many different ways of planting a Three Sisters garden, so don't worry about being too precise about the details. You may prefer to use mounds instead of flat circles for example, or even slight depressions to catch rain if you live in a very dry area.

What you need

- 5 x 10 foot garden area
- Corn, squash and bean seeds

Instructions

1. With a stick, trace out circles that are about 18 inches in diameter. You should have 2 rows of three circles in your 5 x 10-foot garden plot
2. Plant the corn. With a fingertip, make 4 depressions in the soil on the edge of each circle, evenly spaced. Place 2 or 3 seeds in each hole and cover lightly. Water as you normally would after planting seeds. When the plants start to grow, you will keep the strongest 4 and thin out the rest.
3. Plant the squash in 4 places on the inside between the circles. Again, plant a few seeds per hole and thin them later.

4. Once the corn is 6 inches tall, plant the beans on the edge of the circles between the corn plants, 4 per circle. Plant 2 or 3 seeds per hole, and thin later.

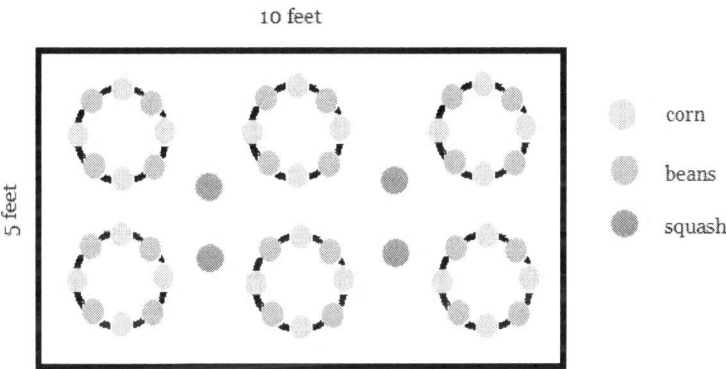

If you plan to eat the beans fresh, keep picking them as soon as they are ready; otherwise the plants will stop producing. Traditionally, the corn and beans would be left to dry on the stalks and then harvested in late fall and stored for the winter.

At the end of the season, leave the roots in the ground to enrich the soil for next year.

A Summer Vegetable Mini-Garden

By staggering your planting times and using compatible plants, you can get a lot of mileage out of a small amount of space. This next garden plan will allow you to grow carrots, lettuce, herbs, tomatoes and a few onions in a 4 x 4 foot plot! The lettuce has shallow roots, so it will not compete with the deep-rooted carrots. The onions take up very little room and help keep pests away. The basil and tomatoes may even improve their yield by growing close together.

Even in this mini-garden, you can plant a variety of different kinds of lettuce, tomatoes and even basil. Diversity means that there's a good chance that at least some of your plants will take off and do really well.

What you need

- 4 x 4-foot garden plot
- Carrot and lettuce seeds
- Onion seedlings

- Tomato and basil seedlings (start them yourself indoors or buy ready for planting from a nursery), 4 of each
- Stakes for tomatoes

Instructions

1. Plant carrot and lettuce seeds in early spring, using the whole garden plot. Add onions here and there.
2. Start basil and tomato plants from seed indoors, unless you plan to buy them at a garden center
3. When it's almost time to plant the basil and tomatoes (check what date is safe for these plants where you live), start harvesting lettuce from the sunniest part of the plot to make room for the basil. Also harvest lettuce and carrots to make four circles of empty space for your tomato plants.
4. Plant tomato and basil plants. Once these plants start to grow, you will have enough ground cover to shade the soil and prevent moisture loss.

The carrots that grow alongside the tomatoes may be a little small, but they will have a great flavor. If your growing season allows it, plant a few more carrot seeds when the tomatoes are starting to reach the end of their life cycle.

Container Gardens

Even if all you have is a balcony or small patio, you can still be a gardener! In addition to flowers, try growing some of these combinations.

Tomatoes are a favorite container plant. If you plant them with a climbing pea or bean, they can share the same trellis and the legume acts as a nitrogen fixer. Plant basil and tomatoes together to improve yield and flavor.

Eggplants grow slowly at the beginning of the season, and then more quickly in the heat of summer. Why not pair them with radishes, which grow quickly in the spring and provide leaf cover to protect the soil and developing eggplant? You can add a tarragon plant too, to repel bugs and stimulate plant growth.

Peppers, both hot and sweet, are also slow-growing early in the season. For this reason, they also work well with radishes.

Bok choy works well with alliums such as garlic, onions or chives. As an added bonus, if you get tired of eating your bok choy, allow it to go to seed and you'll be surprised by its brilliant yellow flowers.

Try planting **climbing peas** in a hanging planter and let them drape instead of climb. Add some French marigolds to the middle of the planter to repel pests.

Strawberries are another popular patio plant. Pair them with lupins, which fix nitrogen, attract pollinators, and add beauty and color to your container garden.

Cucumbers can also work in containers. Look for bush varieties such as Bush Pickle. Plant them with lettuce and radishes and you've got the makings of a great salad.

Chapter 3 – Transitioning to a Companion Garden

Adding Companion Plants to an Existing Garden

If you've already got a well-established garden and you don't want to mess with it too much, you can still benefit from companion planting practices. You can begin the transition towards a companion-planted garden by adding a few beneficial species to your existing garden.

Rather than changing your garden plan in one fell swoop, you can start by working with what you already have. Perennials such as asparagus can benefit from the addition of some companion vegetables and herbs. You can plant flowers and herbs around the borders and between the rows of your garden. Maybe as a first project you can dismantle your onion patch and plant onions amongst your other vegetables. Every year you will get a little more comfortable with companion planting, and you'll become an expert on what works best in your own garden.

It also helps to think outside the box, or the garden plot. You may not think of your raspberry bushes or your crab-apple tree, much less your flower beds, as part of your vegetable garden. But these areas also benefit from companion planting.

Alliums: This is the family that includes onions, garlic and chives. Plant these throughout your garden rather than keeping them all together. They will deter a wide variety of insect pests while at the same time attracting beneficial insects. Just keep them away from beans, peas and sage. Chives produce attractive (and edible) flowers, and can be used in flower gardens too. They are often used to protect roses from black spot, but the chives have to be established for a few years before you'll get results.

Aromatic Herbs: Basil, oregano, mint, dill, rosemary and sage will keep a variety of flying insects at bay, so you can plant them throughout and around your garden. Mint can take over very quickly, so it's best to keep it in a container. Dill should be kept away from carrots.

Marigolds: Plant some of these throughout your garden. You can even scatter the seeds to the wind in early spring and let them pop up where they will. French marigolds in particular produce a natural pesticide in their roots that can keep soil pests such as nematodes at bay. The scent of the marigold plant also deters flying insect pests.

Nasturtiums: These can repel squash bugs, and also act as a trap crop for aphids. You can plant them amongst your squash, or adjacent to the crops that you are trying to protect from aphids. Nasturtiums are beautiful to look at, and are also edible. The peppery leaves and bright flowers add flavor and color to salads.

Radishes: These have a couple of advantages. You can interplant them in your garden because they mature while many of your other plants are still growing. They also act as a trap crop for a variety of insect pests. Little-known fact: radish seed pods are delicious raw or cooked if you pick them green!

Zinnias: Plant some of these colorful annuals around the edges of your garden or between the rows to attract beneficial insects to your garden. Pollinators such as wasps, hover flies and a wide variety of butterflies are attracted to zinnias.

More Tips for Transitioning to Companion Planting

If you have **raspberries**, try planting turnips and garlic near them. Garlic deters fungus and Japanese beetles, while turnips will repel Harlequin beetles.

If you have **asparagus,** you know how long it took you to establish it. It's not going anywhere, but you can plant some tomatoes, parsley and basil around it. Just keep the onions, garlic and potatoes further away.

Do you have **apple** or other fruit trees? Instead of leaving the ground underneath them bare, you can plant herbs such as chives or bee balm. Chives can have the same protecting effect on apples as they do on roses. Bee balm is great for attracting pollinators and other beneficial insects. You can plant flowers such as Echinacea and lupins under fruit trees as well. Echinacea helps make deep soil nutrients more available to the trees, and lupins are nitrogen fixers that also attract butterflies.

Start adding vegetables to your flower beds. Flowering herbs such as chives and oregano are an obvious place to start, but even peppers, eggplants and cherry tomatoes can look attractive in a flower bed. If your flower garden incorporates a fence, use it as a trellis for scarlet runner beans. These edible beans have also long been used as decorative plants because of their brilliant red flowers.

Chapter 4 – Companion Gardening in Perspective

The Science of Companion Gardening

Most of the recommended pairings in companion planting are based on tradition and folklore rather than scientific research. The relationship between science and companion planting has often been rocky. In the 1930s a German soil scientist named Ehrenfried Pfeiffer began advocating for biodynamic agriculture and investigating companion planting. While Pfeiffer had a big influence on the adoption of organic gardening, his theories and methods were grounded in anthroposophy, an early 20th century form of mysticism. He developed a method called "sensitive crystallization" which attempted to link the colors of crystallized plant juices to their status as good or bad companion plants, rather than observing such plants interacting in the real world. Needless to say, most scientists were not impressed. Their rejection of Pfeiffer's theories and methods has led some of them to reject the notion of companion planting out of hand.

It doesn't help that companion planting is so difficult to study scientifically. Scientific studies work by isolating a variable and testing it. Gardens are such complex systems that it's almost impossible to control all of the variables. One study found that tomatoes and basil do combine to produce higher yields, but only if they are planted very densely. If the experimenters had not thought to try a dense planting, they would not have noticed this positive effect and the study could have been interpreted as debunking the idea that basil and tomatoes are good companion crops.

Still, the fact that plants interact with each other is well known to science. Scientists know all about allelopathy, and studies also support the idea that certain plants repel insects and weeds. Nitrogen fixing is undeniable, as is the benefit of growing some crops in the shade of other crops. It's also pretty much undisputed that planting more varieties of plants in the same location makes them less susceptible to pests and disease. The scientific case for companion planting is growing stronger all the time.

It can be frustrating that there are no hard and fast rules for companion planting, but it's easy to see why this is so.

Climate varies from place to place, as do the wild animals and plants that interact with gardens. Soil conditions can vary within a neighborhood, and even your own backyard as different "microclimates". And there are factors (like how densely you plant) that have simply not been passed down in the lore because nobody realized that they were important to the process. Companion planting is still as much an art as it is a science.

When you find conflicting advice, the best thing to do is experiment and find out what works best in your own situation. You may find that you have to start some crops earlier or later than what is recommended, or that two "sworn enemies" like beans and garlic do just fine together in your garden. This unpredictability is part of what makes companion planting so fascinating.

Companion Gardening and Organic Gardening

Organic gardeners do not use any chemical fertilizer or pesticide on their gardens. If you have an organic garden, companion planting will be one of the most useful tools in your toolbox for dealing with pests.

Planting all of your broccoli or potatoes in one place makes it really vulnerable to flying insect pests. A large group of similar plants is really easy for insects to find and attack. If insects have to search through multiple different species to find the right plant for their needs, they are less likely to find your prized crops. You can even distract insects with trap crops, which (if all goes according to plan) the insects will eat while leaving your important plants alone.

Many plants also produce chemicals that repel insects and other pests. And a densely planted companion garden with living mulch is less likely to be taken over by weeds, eliminating the need for weed killing chemicals.

Organic gardeners use compost and manure to fertilize the soil, but using nitrogen fixers also helps in this regard. All in all, it's hard to imagine having a successful organic garden without using some companion planting principles.

You can even grow some plants to make into organic bug sprays for your garden. This doesn't exactly qualify as companion gardening, but it's another way that you can use plants to benefit your crops.

Here is one recipe:

Organic Garden Pest Spray

Ingredients:

- 4 garlic cloves
- 4 hot peppers (such as cayenne or habanero)
- 1 Tbsp liquid castile soap
- 2 Tbsp cooking oil
- 2 ½ cups hot water

Instructions:

1. Blend all ingredients on high for a few minutes.
2. Let stand overnight in a glass or ceramic vessel

3. Strain using a strainer or cheesecloth, and store in a glass jar

To use, put a couple of tablespoons of the mixture into a 16-oz sprayer and use as needed to control insect pests. It's a good idea to wear gloves when handling this mixture, and please be sure not to get it anywhere near your eyes!

And another one:

Basil Tea for Aphids

Ingredients

- 1 cup fresh basil leaves
- 4 cups of water
- 1 tsp liquid castile soap

Instructions

1. Bring the water to a boil. Add basil and remove pot from the heat.

2. Allow the mixture to sit until cooled
3. Strain and stir in liquid castile soap
4. Apply to any garden plants that are infested by aphids

Companion Gardening and Permaculture

Permaculture is an approach to gardening and landscaping that seeks to work with nature rather than against it. The goal is to create self-sustaining mini-ecosystems that produce food and other materials necessary for human life. Permaculture emphasizes choosing plants that are native or well-established in your area. Biodiversity, attracting beneficial insects and other creatures, and sustainability are all part of the permaculture ethos.

It's easy to see how companion gardening fits into this framework. Permaculture gardens imitate nature by planting several different species in the same area. "Stacking" or growing a series of plants with different heights and different light requirements on top of each other, is a form of companion planting used in permaculture.

Permaculture is a philosophy that can become a complete way of life. But many people choose to include some permaculture elements in their own gardens without necessarily adopting the entire lifestyle. Companion planting can be a good first step towards incorporating permaculture techniques in your own garden and life.

Chapter 5 - A Plant-by-Plant Reference Guide

First of all, it's good to be aware of how some common garden plants are related to each other. In many though not all cases, if a plant works well with another plant, it will also work well with other plants of the same family.

Alliums: onions, garlic, chives and leeks

Legumes: Peas, beans, alfalfa, clover

Brassicas: broccoli, cabbage, kale, cauliflower, mustard, turnip

Nightshades: tomato, potato, eggplant, peppers, ground cherries. In most cases it's best to separate these in your garden.

Here are some common garden vegetables, and some guidelines about which plants are the best companions for them. These combinations come from a mixture of tradition, observation, folklore and science. Feel free experiment and see which ones work for your garden.

Alliums

- Good for: brassicas, carrots, tomatoes, potatoes, sweet peppers, fruit trees, roses
- Helped by: tomatoes, carrots, marigolds, mints
- Don't plant with: beans and peas, parsley, sage

Asparagus

- Good for: tomatoes, parsley, strawberries
- Helped by: tomatoes, parsley, dill, basil, marigolds
- Don't plant with: alliums, potatoes

Beans and other legumes

- Good for: almost every garden plant
- Helped by: potatoes, marigolds. Corn acts as living trellis for pole beans
- Don't plant with: alliums

Beets

- Good for: bush beans, brassicas, lettuce, onion

- Helped by: bush beans, lettuce, onion
- Don't plant with: pole beans

Broccoli

- Good for: lettuce
- Helped by: lettuce, beets, carrots, onions, most aromatic herbs, marigolds, nasturtiums
- Don't plant with: strawberries

Cabbages

- Good for: beans and peas, celery, broccoli
- Helped by: alliums, beets, dill, rosemary, sage
- Don't plant with: lettuce, peppers, strawberries

Carrots

- Good for: alliums, beans and peas, tomatoes, lettuce, rosemary, sage
- Helped by: alliums, beans and peas, lettuce, wormwood
- Don't plant with: dill, parsnips

Celery

- Good for: beans and peas, brassicas, cucumber
- Helped by: alliums, beans and peas, tomatoes
- Don't plant with: corn, lettuce

Corn

- Good for: beans and peas (especially climbing beans), cucurbits, tomatoes
- Helped by: beans and peas, soybeans, cucurbits, potatoes, dill, parsley, geraniums
- Don't plant with: celery

Cucumbers

- Good for: beans and peas, lettuce
- Helped by: beans and peas, celery, alliums, radish, marigolds, nasturtiums, dill
- Don't plant with: potatoes (especially late varieties)

Lettuce

- Good for: radishes, beets, beans and peas, onion, broccoli, carrots
- Helped by: beets, beans and peas, broccoli, carrots, cucumber, alliums, strawberries, radishes, cilantro, dill, lavender
- Don't plant with: celery, brassicas, parsley

Peppers:

- Good for: okra
- Helped by: eggplant, beans and peas, brassicas, corn, hemp, marigolds
- Don't plant with: cucurbits, tomatoes, most fruit trees, strawberries, raspberries

Potatoes

- Good for: Brassicas (cabbage, broccoli and family), beans and peas, corn
- Helped by: Alliums, brassicas, legumes
- Don't plant with: asparagus, carrots, cucurbits, tomatoes, strawberries

Strawberries

- Good for: beans, lettuce, onion, spinach, asparagus
- Helped by: beans and peas, caraway
- Don't plant with: brassicas, nightshade family, mint

Squash

- Good for: corn, beans
- Helped by: radish, lavender, marigold, nasturtium
- Don't plant with: potatoes

Tomatoes

- Good for: alliums, asparagus, broccoli, celery, peppers
- Helped by: alliums, basil, carrots, corn, beans and peas, rosemary, sage, parsley, marigolds, nasturtiums
- Don't plant with: potatoes, kohlrabi

Non-Food Plants Used in Companion Gardening

Many of these plants are in fact edible, but they are grown in vegetable gardens primarily to benefit your edible crops.

Amaranth: repels pests such as leaf miners. Plant with corn, onion and potato

Black nightshade: trap crop for potato beetles if planted near potatoes

Calendula: deter a large variety of insect pests and act as a trap crop for others. Plant as a border or throughout your garden

Clover: As a nitrogen fixer, makes a great green manure. Blossoms attract pollinators.

Cosmos: Attracts pollinators while repelling insect pests. Plant around or throughout garden

Geranium: Good for keeping away cabbage worms if planted near cabbage. Also deters Japanese beetles. Plant near corn, tomatoes, cabbage and peppers.

Marigold: French marigolds produce a chemical in their roots that kills nematodes. Marigolds also repel whiteflies. Plant anywhere except with beans.

Nasturtium: An excellent trap crop for black aphids; also deters a wide variety of other pests. Plant just about anywhere in your garden.

Tansy: An effective repellant for many pests, including flies and sugar ants. This is toxic to livestock, so do not plant where animals may be grazing.

Zinnia: These attractive flowers attract hummingbirds and many pollinators. They also make a good trap crop for Japanese beetles. These can be planted as a border or throughout the garden.

Finally, if you enjoyed this book, then I'd like to ask you for a favor, would you be kind enough to leave a review for this book on Amazon? It'd be greatly appreciated!

Thank you and good luck!

Printed in Great Britain
by Amazon